Chance & Choice

New Women's Voices Series, No. 129

poems by

Alice Bolstridge

Finishing Line Press
Georgetown, Kentucky

Chance & Choice

New Women's Voices Series, No. 129

ACKNOWLEDGMENTS

Thanks to publications where poems from this book first appeared.

Wolf Moon Press Journal: "Climbing," "The Garden in Spring," "Sunrise"
Out of Line: "Brooding," "Beyond Belief"
Passager: "CHANCE AND CHOICE." (Passager Poet Award)
Maine in Print: "Are you Happy." (Maine Writers & Publishers' Alliance Poetry Contest,
First Prize)
Nimrod: "Desert Light" (as "Desert Plant"]; "Dr. Wilhelm Reich;" "Voyager;" "Map of
Mammoth Cave" (Finalists, Pablo Neruda Poetry Prize)
Natural Bridge: "Dreaming."
LETTERS TO A LOVER: Gold Wake Press
Animus: "Lawn and Field"
Quantum Tao: "Northern Light"
New Press Literary Quarterly: "Milky Way"
The Maine Scholar: "Mapping Time" [as "Mama Kills Time"]
Oppression for the Heaven of It: "My Son, the Artist." (Winner, 2013 Kenneth Patchen
Award for Experimental Fiction)

Big thanks to my editor Christen Kincaid; to my son Alan Mountain (1956-2015) for
cover art; to photographer Shelly Mountain for the author photo. Thanks to The Taft
Memorial Grant of Cincinnati for three summers of grant funding that allowed time from
teaching at the University of Cincinnati for creative writing projects.

Publisher: Leah Maines
Editor: Christen Kincaid
Cover Art: Alan Mountain
Author Photo: Shelly Mountain
Cover Design: Elizabeth Maines McCleavy

Printed in the USA on acid-free paper.
Order online: www.finishinglinepress.com
                   also available on amazon.com

Author inquiries and mail orders:
Finishing Line Press
P. O. Box 1626
Georgetown, Kentucky 40324
U. S. A.

Table of Contents

For Alan Mountain, "My Son, the Artist" (1956-2015).
And for my daughter and son, Shelly and David.
And for my grandsons, Dylan, Micah,
& Dustin whose birth inspired the poem "Chance & Choice."
And for all people with mental illnesses and their families,
who suffer with courage, inspiration, and hope.

Climbing

I must have climbing genes, an urge
to get to the top of the tallest tree
and see the wider view. As a child,
I did it often: first the stunted dutch apple,
smallest tree in the orchard;
then every tree in the woods
that gave me a foothold; finally to the top
of the old tall pine in front of the house
where I would get drunk with swaying.

But, like Icarus, I like best some of my flight genes
for going aloft. In dream, I stretch out flat,
belly to earth, float up and up until I feel the air
flow over and under me, and I ride
the currents, soaring kin to eagle and hawk.

Or I grow flaps of skin stretching
from thighs to fingertips like a bat.
I bend my knees and flap my arms faster
and faster until I can spring away from the earth.
This flight is harder than floating
or soaring, and I can't get as high.
Though it gives me the brief sweet taste
of nectar, in the end I must brace myself
for the long flight back to the cave.

Awake, I am closest kin to earth-bound
climbers like weasel and wild cat: predator,
egg-eater, crawling along the earth like snake
to search out wild pleasures of meat
and melon and mating.

Brooding.

Careless, I forgot to close the door
to the new tool shed. Next day,
I frightened a robin from the rafter
in the corner. She was building her nest
of mud and wispy brown foliage,
perfect half sphere. So I left the door open
to watch from time to time.

Next time I peered in, she brooded
and stayed steadfast. First chance I got
to find her gone, I climbed on the step stool
to see three small blue eggs, white speckled,
perfect ellipsoids. A few days hence
the brood emerged chirping, mouths gaping.

I visited every day and neglected the noisy
tilling and mowing so as not to disturb them,
waiting to see them fledge.
One day, hardly more than two weeks
from the time I first scared her,
they were all simply gone.

Distracted by early lettuce sprouting
and daffodils blooming in spite
of the late spring, cold and wet,
did I miss their safe flight into the world?
Or was the nest visited in the dark hours
by a weasel or some other climbing creature?

I closed and latched the door, thinking
that was that, and turned to the mowing
and tilling. But late the same day I forgot again.
Next thing I know, she's brooding once more,
two more perfect eggs to hatch.

Beyond Belief

"I saw the barrier of . . . obstinate pride,
and I kept my words safely beyond belief."
(Louise Erdrich. Tracks.)

It's beyond belief, robins brooding
over and over with all the predators
around: snakes, weasels, feral cats, hawks.
Even if they do fledge without mishap, life
is risky, no safety guarantees, no life
or health insurance to save them.

One time, I scared one from her nest
on the rafter in the garage and later
found the eggs on the gravel drive
just outside the door. It looked
as though I interrupted her laying
which couldn't wait.

I find the eggs dropped other places,
one just this morning lying on mulch
under the blooming apple tree, so bright blue
amid the fallen white petals, at first
I thought it was unfound Easter candy.
It's beyond belief—we say it as if

belief were a place on the way to where
you want to go. We must be pointing
out a direction because we aren't robins
who know without doubt to follow
other guides in their brooding.
We care about belief. We marry and divorce

for belief. We surrender our will to Faith
for it. We give away our children
to our country to go warring and dying
for it. We give up joy in blooming
and brooding—our saving joy
beyond doubt, beyond belief—

CHANCE AND CHOICE

1. Birth Cry

I feared my fear of life and death would blind
me so I couldn't see my grandson's birth
16 weeks early. A fetus this fragile,
law and choice allows, is not enough alive
or human to bear the right of life.
But, almost against my will, I glanced
and saw, squeezed into folds like a raw brain,
                    the glistening crown.

Then I couldn't look away.
The head emerged, it breathed, it cried,
a mewl softer than a new-born kitten's.
He slid out. I reached to touch.

His hand, tiny as a baby eagle's claw,
curled 'round my finger, clutched.

2. Chance

Within minutes of his birth, his mother
had to choose. Resuscitate or not?
Without it, he would die, *mercifully*
many said. With it, tubes would invade him
again and again—through nose, mouth, veins
and arteries. 50% chance he might die anyway;
of those who live, more than 30% have some degree
of life-time handicap—blind, retarded, palsied.

90% have major complications.
The only certainties—quick death if *no*,
months-long suffering and disease if *yes*.
She didn't hesitate—*help him live*.

Amid high-tech glare and urgency,
a tracheal tube cut off his cry.

3. Desire

Her first baby. She'd never seen one
so small, so fully formed a human he seemed
a freak at 1 ½ pounds, seemed too delicate
to bear the sound of his own heartbeat.
Knowing the chances, what compelled, at sight
and sound of him, her unthinking yes?

Her hand covered his whole back, she stroked
and murmured. Not able to hold him for weeks,
she yearned to put his whole foot in her mouth,
the mammal's urge to lick, the human kiss.

What but desire too deep in our animal brain
to voice, unspeakable joy, skin to skin.

4. Choice

Nature documents animal drives:
several mother elephants struggle
in concert to save an adopted baby mired
in mud; in drought, a whole herd
halts its way to water and waits

in dust swirls for one mother nuzzling
one new baby, urging its pained effort
to rise on defective legs; they caress
a dead companion's carcass while scavengers
eat and flesh turns to liquid, dissolves
into earth. They carry the bones like babies,
rocking foot to foot. Animals

all, hanging on the cross of life and death
together, we get to choose surrender.

5. Hush

A nurse explained it is used universally,
the sound the placenta makes working
at fetal feeding. It's also the sound
of breath, mother's milk gushing,
the dark behind her baby's fused eyes,
his gaze when he opens them.

It's the sound of breezes and mist, sunlight,
microbes and worms working compost
into soil, water in the deepest currents.
It's the sound of sorrow's ebb tide.

To our feet, our rage, and our suffering,
the earth, our placenta, sings *shh*.

The Garden in Spring

In the beginning, when Adam awoke
and first saw the garden all blooming
and pastel green like here, did he ache
like this with the beauty of blossom
and apple and tree?

Or, was he one like some
born blind and suddenly restored to sight,
so pained by vision they refuse to see?
Did he cover his eyes with his hands?
Close them tight against the light?

Or did he delight in vision from the beginning?
Did he go about the naming in an ecstasy
of seeing, outlines of difference emerging
out of the blur, distinctions growing sharper,
clearer, smaller and smaller: forest, tree,
flower, bee, gold pollen grains on white petals?

Or was it only after the naming frenzy
that he found fault with creation. He had God
and the whole garden—lavish with difference,
with presence—all to himself,
but he saw absence, yearned for a mate.

When he awoke to find Eve, did he see her
beauty from the beginning: short,
hair streaming out away from her small face
in the wind, fleshy round breasts
between narrow shoulders, wide hips,
and the thatch between her legs
with its peculiar absence.

Did he see her beauty at home
in the garden, bending down to gather
lettuce, new onions, and thyme gone wild?
Or was he more intent
on the ache of his missing rib?

Human from the beginning,
not divine, and becoming more distinct
from each other with each day,
did Adam and Eve together have to wait
for their bliss until after the fall
with its news of dying blazing
across the maple forests?
Did they have to wait
until after the fall and
long winter of knowing?

Are You Happy?

Eve in Paradise to Adam:
"How are we happy, still in fear of harm?"
John Milton. Paradise Lost.

1.
Water from the artesian well
overflows and collects in a pool.
We kneel, drink deep.
Oh, happy moment!

2.
Be here now. Certainly.
Smell the blossoming lilac.
Snuggle with your beloved.
In the garden, eat
the sun-warmed tomato.
Cherish the moment.

3.
No zealots among the vulnerable
tulips. Forgive them their gaudy dress.
Lacking the shame of moral thought,
they flirt out their brief lives.

4.
Little yellow finches flit
through the poplars
and sing, Nature's spoiled
children protected from
the Tree of Knowledge.
They yield themselves
               to Paradise.

5.
Child-animal,
think,
become human.
Oh, loss! Oh, hunger!
            Bless us.

6.
　　　Adam was led by lofty senses
of obedience to the eternal.
Eve was the one swayed by delight
in the ephemeral, the one to look
with longing. Thus they rebelled
against the only commandment
in Eden. Surely a merciful law
in view of what God knew
about all that would come after.

7.
Juice was sweet on her tongue, dripping
down her chin, when she kissed him.
She brought the dewy fruit
to their mouths. They chewed and licked
until their whole bodies were drenched
in the juices, until the sweetness coursed
through their blood, until it pierced the DNA.

8.
Even at that, could we not have been saved
if she had not said, *See how good?*
　　　We will not surely die?
if he had not stopped then
　　　to think of eternity,
if they had not hurried
to gather the leaves?

9. after Mary Oliver's "Morning Poem:"
        The rapist pulls
        the world down
        into a heap of olive leaves.
        Black-painted lilies
        block the trails
        leading to the wells.
                Pray.

10.
What to do the with that pile
of moments that became history?
What to do with the burning eyes
approaching the rose?

11.
Are you happy? In the after myths
of Eden, struggle through
the painted lilies, the cult-
ivation. At the wells, drink deep,
watch the finches, fill buckets
        with water for your gardens.

Desert Light

He tells me it's a curious desert plant
that resists cultivation, grows without care.
Trembling, I take his hand to follow
into wild places without paths,
maps, memories, or myths to guide us,
with only the sun ahead and the wind
filling our footsteps with sand behind.
He pauses, hesitates. I push on
and lose myself so
       I don't see when my hand
leaves his and I lose him and forget
the rare plant we set out to find.

Light pushed beyond shadow's range
loses itself in its own radiance.

Dreaming

I dream of his dream of a woman
conceived in some strain of his thigh.
Expansive as a prairie, he lies
stretched in his labored coming.

She appears first as a slight swelling
where his thigh is bent as though broken.
It heads slowly, ruptures, spills
white down his leg. She comes

through the wound, wet, long hair like
cocoon silk wrapping her round. She shakes
and quakes to dry until her hair fans out
like blue dragonfly wings, and she rises

and turns to face him, her beloved beast
conceived in some strain that still aches.

Dr. Wilhelm Reich

Dr. Wilhelm Reich thought erotic energy
divine—gluey stuff that holds the universe.
He named it *orgone*, boxed it, shipped it
across state lines to heal the world.
The food and drug people judged him
        cracked and jailed him.

But, felt as some sense, it must be beyond
the range of mind, like sound frequencies
elephants or dogs or moose can hear,
but too low or high for us. Installing
moose alerts on my car, I imagine
my skin rising to unheard song. As water
rises toward the moon, so blood must rise
        to what we cannot know . . . .

LETTERS TO A LOVER

1.

All this letter crossing,
reading you to me on my way to you,
makes me dizzy, like whirling
when we were kids until disoriented
and staggering.

Meaning slips. What the poem meant
when I observed its source, is not the same thing
I meant when I wrote it (1st, 2nd, 3rd, 4th drafts;
then I lost count as I stopped keeping new drafts),
is not what I meant when I wrote of it
in a snit to a critical reader,
is not what I mean as I write this letter,
will not be what I mean when I read it
tomorrow, etc. Meaning
dissolves before the message arrives.

2.

Life is in the shifts and trans-
formations. A totally new and different body
every seven years, cellular decay
and renewal. Which is why
I define all the time, everything.
Did I say I'm dizzy?

Worshippers of Saraswati, Hindu Goddess
of knowledge and creativity,
ritually throw exquisitely modeled,
unfired clay images of her into the river
to dissolve back into the elements.

3.

At a workshop in silent meditation,
our clowning teacher gives us a ball of clay,
tells us to fully express our whole selves
in an image. Half way through he tells us
to ball it all up and start over.
I say *ouch* aloud, breaking the rules again.
But I destroy it anyway.

Now, I don't even remember
what the first image was that pained me so
to let go. And then I cheated again,
kept the second image, a hand
reaching out of a whirlpool,
until, in one of my moves, it got lost or broken.

4.

With their slow, sure power, tugboats
on the Ohio River haul or push
huge barges while many small speedboats zoom
up and down and across the river.

I'm caught in a whirling current more powerful
than desire. I stepped in, thinking
I could swim a bit with it.
But then it takes over,
and I fear for my power of any choice.

I reach out to a speedboat, but I'm too slow.
It zooms right on by, and a tugboat

way down the river comes toward me
making such a racket with its bass rumble,
with its slow sure power,
it drowns out the sound of speedboats
near by and mutes my own soundings.

There's a beached hulk just ahead; maybe
I could reach it, latch on.   The tugboat
has turned away leaving a wake
of phantom pain.

5.

Cincinnati is lovely today in the rain,
only three days of sunshine in May.
The heat has not arrived, and it is green all over,
hundreds of shades of green
in all the parks and wooded areas.
Tulips, jonquils, and lilac are mostly gone,
A small purple flower smells sweet,
and our letters still veer back and forth
between "to be continued" and "the end."

Lawn and Field

I take a common walk across a lawn
where even the grass is hushed,
too low to blow in the breeze

to a field beyond where commotion
rules. Insects buzz, flutter, click,
chirp. Birds sing. Wind whistles

through grass and saplings. Flowers riot.
Seeds rattle in dry pods. Everywhere,
the fecund wild reclaims the land.

A fox staggers out of the woods,
stops, hunches, bares its teeth
through foaming drool, rabid.

The always something everywhere
wilder than grass or sex or death.

Northern Light
at a Scandinavian Art Show

The light of "Midnight Sun"
shines green, red, and gold
on hard matter—a cliff,

a building, a boat. A distant
late sun colors the sky and water
the black-blue of a fresh bruise.

In the center foreground, white
water rushes to a still black pool.
It all goes to stillness

like color of the aurora borealis—
light that can mass, or band, or stream,
but always moves to still dark.

Charged particles, physicists
think. I like to know the physics—
magnetic fields and lines of force

that explain the north's attraction,
storms of charge and counter charge
that keep it all moving, matter

that cannot hold. I'd even like
to know the weight of light. But more,
I wonder at the drawing of life

to still life and midnight to dawn.

Milky Way

With the right perspective,
it looks like a whirlpool of light.
At midnight, far from summer,

lying flat on my back in snow,
no moon, I watched it, all
black and white. I watched

until I saw the stars move
across the wide arc of sky,
until I felt myself move

in a slow whirl with earth
in heaven. I breathed
into the cold dark and felt

my body warming that whole
field of snow. And still
I watched until I saw radiant

energy whirl dew through
the air, warm milk swirl
through flesh, nipple to mouth,

and blood, Ishmael watching a lance
cut the teats of a nursing whale.
Milk and blood pour and swirl.

Between earth and the stars,
the dark heaves with the heat of it.
It warms the cosmic cold.

Map of Mammoth Cave

When I got home, I studied the map to see
the shape of where we'd been—
a closed loop, in and down, up and out.
We took the Historic Entrance to The Rotunda
where the ceiling swirled from an ancient
whirlpool and space dwarfed our community,
a guide and 123 strangers.
Broadway to the amphitheater where Booth
did Shakespeare before he undid Lincoln.
The guide turned off the lights for absolute
dark and threw flaming torches on to the stage
to show how his drama was lit. Gothic Avenue
to Giant's Coffin—half of the tour done.
I wanted to go on to see the Tuberculosis Huts
in the cavern just beyond, but someone said
Assassination and a coffin are enough.

Then we entered snug spaces. We had to duck
our heads for the passage with no name
on this map, and at Fat Man's Misery
we walked sideways. It was wide though
compared to trips in some wild caves, following
other guides, crawling through mud and water,
neck twisted painfully to keep our noses
in the narrow space of air. Even that
must have been spacious compared to birth.
After a bathroom stop, we sprawled in Great Relief.

At River Hall we heard water running
in the River Styx on the bottom level
where we couldn't go. *Mammoth Cave is dry
and fixed*, the guide said, *except for rare
breakdowns, and except for places like Frozen*

Niagara where formations grow from water
dripping, and except for the bottom level
where, as the water table drops, the river
carves the cave deeper into the limestone.

Many exceptions it seems to me.
At our last stop, Mammoth Dome rose high
over the Ruins of Karnak. Climbing stairs
back to the first level, I lagged behind
thinking how hard it is to get to bottom
and top levels, so I didn't see much
from Little Bat Avenue to Audobon
and back to The Rotunda.

Over 300 miles of the Mammoth System
charted, but 32 times the map
breaks away. Unexplored tunnels lead
to more caverns and levels and dead-
ends. I'd like to see the Egyptian Karnak.
I'd like to see back and back. But, children
in old snapshots, our own parents are strangers.
And grandparents, dying in TB sanitariums
before we were born, are faded brown tintypes
in torn albums. Turning to earth, we must be
like unfixed water, born and reborn to shaping
our shaper and blind to the shape. I study
the cave, wondering how we might get a boat down
to the Styx and row out into the Green River.

Mapping Time

Mama says, *Time goes by, and we go with it.*
If only we had free time, we say, time
to spend like sweepstakes cash, waste
like childhood summer in unmown hay fields,
or fill like a giant balloon with helium
until it lifts us so far up we see the whole
earth round, and we ride the air
like Pegasus, winged and rocking, care
                                                        free.

But carnal rhythms of mortality measure
our animal time: breath, the heart's iambic
dah dub, dah dub, dah dub. Climbing, sex,
                        dancing remind us.
Mama's not dancing much now. She says,
The spirit is willing but the flesh is weak.
Her heart fibrillates. *I feel it fluttering,*
she says, wild. Dear Mama, is your time running
out? She kills time, watches TV all day, sometimes
half the night: news, soaps, nature documentaries.
She swears at the president and gossips
of a personal past that echoes this public heartbreak,
this hunger for sex and power, this greed
to seem good, this rise and fall of righteousness.
                        The wake of Genesis.

The truth is hard to find, and harder to bear.
A surgeon cut out all the cancer he could see,
a section of colon, 30 lymph nodes, 17
malignant. There is more, he's sure, hidden,
waiting. She's too old, her heart too erratic,
the oncologist says, for more treatment.
She mutters, *I know my own body.*
You don't. I'll live to be a hundred. More gentle

now than when, more than 2 decades ago,
she had a breast cut out: advanced cancer.
Then the doctor said a year, maybe 2.
And she said *I'll live to see you dead.* She did.
Further back, she outlived tuberculosis, polio,
hemorrhaging, sputtering through it all
of transgression. We don't talk of our own.

She's almost enough to make me believe
in Pegasus or streets of gold she says
her God has promised she'll have for dancing
in Heaven. *It will be here on earth,* she says.
        We'll come back after the judgment.
Almost enough to make me believe
an infinite measure of time is granted us
        in some dimension I can't know.

I can only see time from birth to death
mapped by linear progression, one
relentless forward thrust. And after, no
redeeming judgment, no ghostly stuff
of us coming back, nor going on.
I can't see the curve of Space-Time on which
a spirit might ride: come back to meet itself
on the other side without ever passing
over the edge like a mobius strip
with its mysterious twist; or loop across
itself like *the lounging eight of infinity;*
or miss itself on its loop around and spiral
out and out, or in and in and take the shape
of a galaxy swirling into a black hole
that sucks away all this dross of deception
and woe and leaves us shining on the far side,
purely true and holy.

My Son, the Artist

In 1976, he sat at the table, unmoving
eyes focused on a spot above
and behind my left shoulder
and talked of the journey
he was taking. A long journey,

he said, on a ship he must pilot
alone through treacherous waters.
He said he was called to go,
he wanted to go, he might not come back.
He did not call me *Mother.*

As I did when he was small
in another hospital room,
frightened that he was dying,
I gave him water colors, ink,
and paper and told him to paint.

In 1979, he neither talked nor listened
to me. Recovering again, his painted
faces split, crumbled, fell and scattered
in pieces on bright tile. Blood streamed
from Christ's heart. In 1984, sometimes

he brought me up to date on the progress
of his journey. Twice, playing his flute,
he said he heard dolphins sing.
Then he seemed close by. In 1999,
back home now for five years,

he greets the millennium with loud laughs
at jokes he says God tells him. He no longer
talks of journeying. Again and again,
he says he is sorry for the costs
of his disease. He gives me a gold-plated

needle—emblem of mending, tribute
to my love of needle work—and a note,
Take the best they gave you and leave
the rest to the devil to carry away into hell,
or wherever he does the dirty work of God,

who I often call the great flipped blip.
And I can't forget before all the sickness,
four years old, a hot summer afternoon,
he told me he was inventing a giant bathtub
with a fountain at the faucet end,

always spraying cool water, always full,
always draining, always flowing clean water;
he drew pictures and explained how water
stayed clear by filtering through
a network of gold piping arching the tub.

Rodin's Fugitive Love

Her upper body freed from the stone,
she swims face down through air
away from him, graceful as a dolphin.
He's overturned, supported on her back,
and facing up in pained surprise.

Feet caught fast as hers in the same stone,
legs straining and twisted, he reaches
over his head and tries to grasp her.
Back-handed, he clutches air.

Camille Claudell, did he drive you crazy,
seeing only the commercial and esthetic
possibilities in you that excited his passion,
a business man like him who sells
his Kiss for a handsome profit?
Or did he, like a Renaissance lover
or Narcissus, gaze into the liquid
surfaces of your eyes and fall in love,
genuinely, with the bottomless dark?

New Orleans Art in July

Surreal erotica of Edward Douillet
reminded me of Bosch; a portrait
of Ernest Hemingway was priced at $7500;
and a book, *A Ballad of Sexual Dependence:*
Photographs of an Extended Family,
displayed bodies in sexual poses.
Some turned their faces away, others faced
forward sulking. Or was that a pout of desire?
One laughed wide, mouth curving
up over gray teeth.
                              Then suddenly
on the next page, just her face,
the photographer's, filled the whole page,
bruised around both eyes. One scarlet eye
stared. I closed the book hard and hurried—
I think I must have hurried—
out into Royal Street toward the sound
of the blues.
                    I found myself
sitting on the curb, praying a counterpoint
to his song. He looked down at his folk
guitar, cracked and mended with masking tape.
Absorbed, face pained, eyes closed, he moaned,
My waiting woman.
                              His percussion player
pounded her washboard and cowbells
and danced, her thin body straining
toward him. Spectators watched, sitting
or standing, leaning against café walls
and light poles, restraining
shoulder sways and hip thrusts,
sweating, each in our own wet heat.

Sunrise

"The thing as in itself it really is"
is just the earth in this spot
here and now
turning toward the sun,

not an omen to sailors of storms—
though they will come, and likely
today—nor of resurrection
no matter how urgent my need
to believe.

       Even so, I sit with pen
and paper—there must be a poem
in this—recording black clouds
with fiery underbellies shifting
to orange, paling and thinning
until the whole sky has turned
all blue and white and gold.
I grab the camera, run outdoors,
try and try to frame the image
of just this thing.

Voyager

It all turns beyond sight
in wide spaces of dark.
Voyager confirmed it, no life

found anywhere else in our solar system.
Mercury and Venus
are too hot, Mars too cold,

Pluto too distant. And the rest
are all just gas—
Jupiter, Saturn, Uranus, Neptune,

each burning in its own
internal combustion,
beautiful as belief,

but life is only here.
An expense of desire
in wide spaces of dark,

it all turns beyond sight
as we in the night turn
from our solitary dreaming

to face each other, belly
to belly, breath to breath,
hot and wet, an expense

of desire. Groping
beyond sight in wide spaces
of dark, we turn

and turn like an infant's head
seeking the nipple,
seeking a place to latch on

and hold, a place where,
caught up beyond sight,
we are blind to the dark.

Alice Bolstridge, Ph. D in English Literature from Oklahoma State University, has spent her professional life teaching literature and writing. In retirement, she advocates for peace and justice issues and teaches Senior Education classes as a volunteer.

Mother of 3 with 3 grandsons, Alice lives in Presque Isle, Maine, the far north of Maine near the Canadian border where night comes down at 4:00 PM in December, and where the shapes and rhythms of shadow and dark inspire dreams of flight into the long-day light of summer. At 79 years old she still experiments with the limits and possibilities of language to illuminate the depths and heights of human experience, to speak the unspeakable. She writes to listen; to pray and wonder; to explore the world; to pretend.

www.ingramcontent.com/pod-product-compliance
Lightning Source LLC
LaVergne TN
LVHW051610080426
835510LV00020B/3226